WATER

A Buddy Book

by

Julie Murray

ABDO
Publishing Company

VISIT US AT
www.abdopublishing.com

Published by ABDO Publishing Company, 4940 Viking Drive, Edina, Minnesota 55435.

Copyright © 2007 by Abdo Consulting Group, Inc. International copyrights reserved in all countries. No part of this book may be reproduced in any form without written permission from the publisher. Buddy Books™ is a trademark and logo of ABDO Publishing Company.

Printed in the United States.

Series Coordinator: Sarah Tieck
Contributing Editor: Michael P. Goecke
Graphic Design: Maria Hosley
Cover Photograph: Photos.com
Interior Photographs/Illustrations: Media Bakery, Photos.com

Library of Congress Cataloging-in-Publication Data

Murray, Julie, 1969–
    Water / Julie Murray.
        p. cm. — (First science)
    Includes index.
    ISBN-13: 978-1-59679-832-8
    ISBN-10: 1-59679-832-7
    1. Water—Juvenile literature. I. Title. II. Series: Murray, Julie, 1969- First Science.

QC145.24.M87 2006
553.7—dc22
                                                                    2006017160

TABLE OF CONTENTS

A WATERY WORLD

Water is a big part of everyday life. Look around. People drink water. The oceans are filled with water. And, water helps farmers grow crops. It is easy to see water in use in many places.

Water is important to life on Earth.

WHY IS WATER IMPORTANT?

Water is the key to life on Earth. Every living thing needs water.

Water helps keep people's bodies healthy. More than half of a person's body is made of water. So, people need to drink water to stay alive.

People use water to take showers and brush their teeth. They also use water for cooking. One person can use about 100 gallons (380 L) of water each day.

People use water to do jobs around the house, such as washing dishes.

When it doesn't rain enough, machines help plants get the water they need to grow.

Water is also used for many important jobs in the world. Farmers use it to grow crops. Factories use it to help make things. Ships carry materials across oceans, rivers, and lakes.

Water is important in nature, too. It helped make the world's mountains and canyons. And, water is the reason we have different types of weather, such as rainstorms.

THE SCIENCE OF WATER

Water is a form of **matter**. All forms of matter are made up of **atoms**. Atoms are very small. Each atom has a **nucleus** at its center.

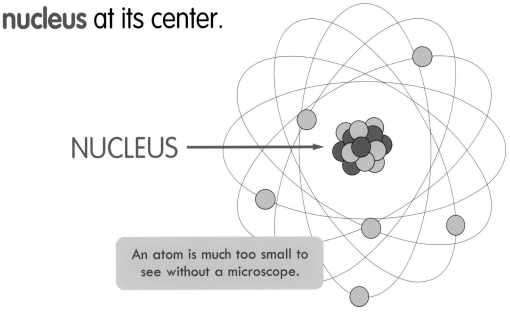

NUCLEUS

An atom is much too small to see without a microscope.

Different kinds of **atoms** can join together. This is called linking. When they link, they form bonds and change. These linked atoms are called molecules.

Water molecules are made up of **hydrogen** and **oxygen**. When two hydrogen atoms join with one oxygen atom, they make water. So, water's scientific name is H_2O. This refers to its chemical make-up.

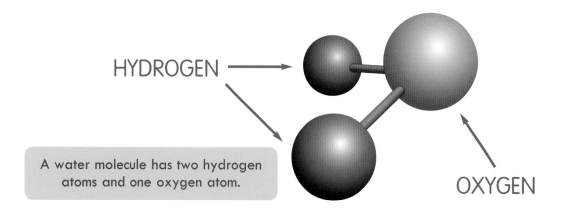

HYDROGEN

A water molecule has two hydrogen atoms and one oxygen atom.

OXYGEN

Water is important both to people and to animals.

THE WATER CYCLE

   Water molecules are recycled in the world. This is because water can appear in solid, liquid, and gas forms. It is one of the only substances on Earth to have this special quality.

   Water in the liquid form is found in the world's oceans, lakes, and rivers.

Rivers have liquid water.

When the sun shines on ocean water that water can **evaporate**. Then it becomes water vapor. Plants can also produce water vapor. Water vapor, or steam, is the gas form of water.

Water vapor eventually comes back to Earth in the form of rain. Sometimes, the water freezes and comes to Earth as snow. Ice and snow are the solid forms of water. This form is also found in glaciers.

The water cycle is important. It helps keep the Earth and the people who live on Earth healthy. The water cycle helps distribute fresh water around the world.

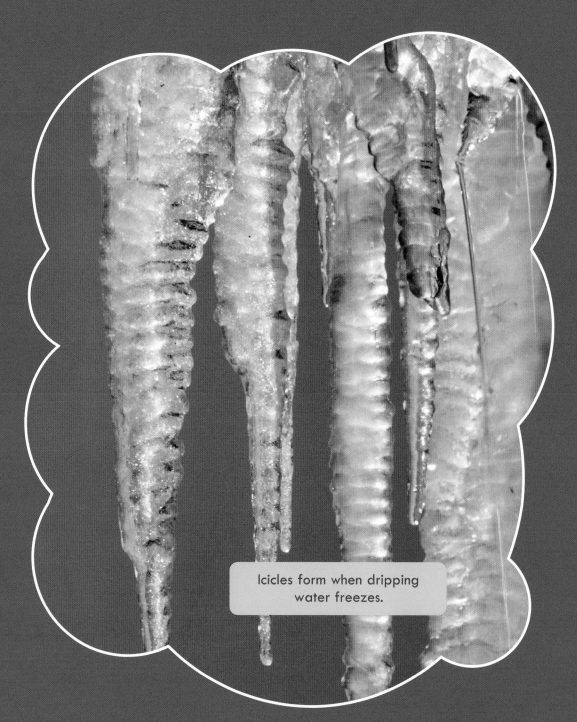

Icicles form when dripping water freezes.

Did you know that water helps make newspapers? It takes about 80 gallons (300 L) of water to make just one Sunday edition of a newspaper.

Recycled paper and wood chips are broken down. A manufacturing plant creates **pulp** using a chemical process. The pulp is mixed with water. Then, the wet mixture is poured onto a special screen to dry. Next, machines help make the dried pulp into paper.

When the paper is ready, it is put on a roll. Then, it is sent to a printing plant. The printer prints the news onto the paper. Then, they cut and fold the pages.

Machines make pulp into large rolls of paper.

WATER THROUGH HISTORY

Through the years, many scientists have studied water. Some have explored the question of where water came from. No one knows for sure how it began.

Still, scientists have made many important discoveries about water. And, most agree there is still more to learn about how water works within our world.

Waterfalls are part of nature.

WATER IN THE WORLD TODAY

Water is a big part of daily life. Without water, people couldn't exist. Without water, the Earth wouldn't have oceans or air.

Water covers about 70 percent of the Earth's surface.

People and animals have
many uses for water.

The world would be a very different
place if there was no water.

.∎ IMPORTANT WORDS ∎.

atom a tiny particle that makes up matter.

evaporate to change into vapor from a liquid or a solid.

hydrogen an element in gas form.

matter what things are made of.

nucleus the center of an atom.

oxygen a colorless and odorless element that is found in water.

pulp a soft, wet mass made by grinding things up.

∎ WEB SITES ∎.

To learn more about **Water**, visit ABDO Publishing Company on the World Wide Web. Web site links about **Water** are featured on our Book Links page. These links are routinely monitored and updated to provide the most current information available.

www.abdopublishing.com

INDEX